FINISHING LINE PRESS

www.finishinglinepress.com

The Leper Dreams of Snow

poems by

Sean Corbin

Finishing Line Press
Georgetown, Kentucky

The Leper Dreams of Snow

ACKNOWLEDGMENTS

The author wishes to thank the following for their support: Amanda Kelley
Corbin, Walter and Sandy Corbin, April and Shane Walters, Crystal Wilkinson,
George Eklund, Chris Prewitt, Ben Whisman, Brent Taylor, and his faculty
and peers at Morehead State University and the University of Kentucky.

Publisher: Leah Maines
Editor: Christen Kincaid
Cover Art: Sean Corbin
Author Photo: Amanda Kelly Corbin
Cover Design: Elizabeth Maines McCleavy

Printed in the USA on acid-free paper.
Order online: www.finishinglinepress.com
          also available on amazon.com

Author inquiries and mail orders:
Finishing Line Press
P. O. Box 1626
Georgetown, Kentucky 40324
U. S. A.

Table of Contents

for Amanda

WANTING TO HELP

What can I do to help I want to ask   *just take it easy*
I expect to hear   *don't strain yourself   don't do too*

much   don't get stressed   don't worry   I worry
I can't help but worry   can't help but try to help with

anything and then just as easily can't help failing to help
if I could help you understand by behaving like a swan

I would   I would hold my wings high above my long
neck and shield the sun from your eyes   I would
flap them to cool your cheeks   I would stretch them

wide to glide over you and block the pouring rain   I
could help if I were a bird   sometimes I feel instead

like a rock resting at the bottom of a muddy basin
unable to help   unable to imagine helping   unable

THE LEPER LOVES

I love how my son's hairline reaches to the top of his scalp
and swoops down like a raven's wing   love the taste of
hazelnuts in my coffee and chocolate   love the air around
a lake after a storm   love the woods after dawn   love how
a high-end bourbon feels on my tongue   love my wife's
hand on my shoulder   love my wife's hand on my chest
love my wife's hand on the telephone or bathroom sink
or the arm of the couch   love my boy's method of
sneak-farting on my leg   love how a butterfly can look
like a mushroom cloud   love a thick steak and a thin beer
love an ink pen and a new sketch pad   love a light   love
a moon   love a blanket of stars in the country   love the
city's electricity   love myself rarely   love myself
spitefully   love myself just enough to keep breathing

SKIN

Melanin makes for feeble arguments   all lip skin
is a shade of pink   I kiss the cracks   I lick the
curves   every supple bump is universal   I want

to love like a leper   like love is falling off of me
like love is tearing me apart   I want to love like
love is too heavy for my bones   I want to settle

into the red blood of every single human being
to let it pump in my veins and yours   I want to love
like a frog leaping from pad to pad   like love is a

spring in my thighs   like love is a surface on which
to land   I hear the pounding sound in my ear
it is not a war drum   it is a heartbeat.

THE LEPER WATCHES *THE ELEPHANT MAN*

I turn up my glass of whiskey   kiss the sun
that burns through the living room window

and spreads into spectrums   the television is
burning in monochrome   John Merrick is on

the screen   twisted and gnarled as his face is
I see my own in the shine of his humps   his

boiling forehead   his curdled bones   he
brings a pair of opera glasses to his eyes and

enjoys civilization   I eat potato chips and
drink more whiskey and burn   I burn

oh god   I burn beneath the bright lights and
think of lying down   and drinking one more

THE LEPER DREAMS OF SNOW

Flakes the size of baseballs float down upon
the ground and gravel drive of an apartment that
is no longer mine   I stand on the porch craving

apricots   no one wants to travel   my sons lie
asleep in their beds   my wife flat-out refuses
my mother and sister say no   and then my dead father

arrives beside the railings on a chestnut-colored horse
he motions for me to follow and begins leading the
horse through the snow   I walk behind him

waiting for a word   waiting for a conversation
something warm from his mouth   he rides in silence
not as if he has nothing to say   but more like what

he wants to say has frozen in his throat   so he presses
through the shoulder-high drifts of snow   showing me
instead how to find something sweet in the winter

THE GRUDGE

What I grip when flood waters rush over me   what I wrap around
my waist when the helicopter nears   what I drape across my

shoulders while the moon emits its icy breath   what I squeeze
between my fingers as the fire ants float past   what I spit heat over

when the floods recede   what I return to on dry land
what I drown in when I cannot forgive the rain

SNEAKING A CHEESEBURGER

I sneak a cheeseburger on my way to work   it expresses itself
in grease and juices across my teeth and tongue   its cheese
coats my gums   it holds me close to its breast and sings

while I drift off into warm beef-fueled meditation   for a
moment I forget my urge to cry   for a moment I forget
the pains in my head   the strange skip in my chest   the

pressure in my muscles   all the while my liver expresses
disbelief at yet another disrespect   later my wife finds the
wrapper in the car   she asks me seventeen questions about

the quality of the patty   whether its buns were better
than hers   I feign ignorance   pretend it is older than it is
I go to sleep on the couch   ashamed of my betrayal

THE LEPER WANTS TO FLY

I paint birds with endless curves   birds
with their wings bent in loops   making
Mobius strips   making infinity   I wish

I had a pet peacock so that I could be the
one to set it free   to let it strut its plumage
around the neighborhood and caw my name

in celebration   I wish I had the stomach
to leap from my roof with my arms stretched
out   my feathers smooth and glistening in

the cool autumn sun   my feet ready for
contact with the trees   heels down   I wish
there was a way to get a wing transplant

I'd trade this dead liver for a single puff
of down   and hold on to it as I fell
screaming toward the hard earth

THE MOON ACROSS THE SUN

Blot out the sun   cast a ring around
the earth   pull the oceans toward

the vacuum of black ink   make me
crazy in my blood and bones   I'll

look at you   burn my retinas for you
thank you for the scars that will forever

remind me of how lucky I am to see you
I'll beg you to fall upon me in full force.

THE LEPER'S SON

I hear my son's footsteps upstairs as early
morning turns late   and remember not

defending him when his cousin was being
mean   not making things equal   not caring

for his heart the way I want mine to be
cared for   and for all the blue pills and pink

pills and white pills that I pop each day I haven't
found the one that treats Failing Father's

disease   haven't found the injection that might
make me more aware of a yell before it crests

over my teeth   haven't found the liquid gel cap
to soothe my acidic control issues   and I don't

want my son to be like me   fragile like a
house made of sawdust   but I don't want him

to be a toothpick either   sharp on either end
and lacking in flexibility   I want him to be

a slap bracelet   formable and fun but with
just enough sting to make his feelings heard

I want him to be just stubborn enough
like me to know he'll never be like me

SHOPPING AT THE GROCERY

There is potential in the aisles and shelves   I could have
anything   I could eat or drink anything   I could be

anything if I just have this certain brand of peanut butter
my wife thinks I'm obsessed   thinks I can't help going

and spending too much money   chalks it up to hypomania
I think of it as steak-mania or shrimp-mania or ice-

cream-and-pasta mania   a madness caused by too much of a
good thing   and it's not that I'm crazy about food so much

as it is that I'm crazy for a place that has everything   a place
that fulfills my needs   a place that satisfies my hunger

a place that fills that emptiness in my stomach with carbs and
flesh   a place that makes me feel   for a time   complete

THE LEPER'S APPROACH TO GRADUATE SCHOOL

I take a chalice made of plutonium   fill it
with my dark diseased piss   leave it

to putrefy for two years   then take a deep drink
and spit it out   angry that it isn't chardonnay

LIFE CHANGES

Today I start a diet of wood chips
and teriyaki sand   of dry leaves

and tree bark   of stagnant water
and stale earthworms for protein

I plan on picking up heavy cinder
blocks and tossing them down into

my father's swimming pool until
my veins rupture   plan on sprinting

from the wind and chasing cars and
barking until the white coats come

plan on doing jumping jacks on the
roof of my convertible and planks on

the backs of my sons until my spine
makes a fist   plan on curling the dog

and squatting the wife until my legs
sprout branches   plan on barrel-rolling

over every tall weed in my backyard
until my calves mow the lawn themselves

I want to glisten in moonlight like a small
creek drifting across smooth stones

I want to ripple when I want to
and not just when poked

THE LEPER CELEBRATES HIS WIFE'S RAISE

I'll stop to get a six-pack of something cash green   I'll
bring it through the door and hold out its carton for her to

choose the bottle that best represents her emotions   I hope
she chooses the one out front   the one leading the charge

of the glass brigade   we'll sit and eat chicken dinner and
talk about her newfound zeroes as if we'd stumbled upon

an excess donut factory   we'll eat white meat and sip hops
and discuss all the things we can strive for now   all

of the mobility we'll upwardly churn   my contribution
a series of changed diapers and poems to sell for grass seed

my raise the one I give to the bottle   its lip on mine   its
organs flowing into my organs   we'll give a toast to

our children and the health care they'll have for their organs
perhaps we'll play the organ in the church of the lower

middle class as the congregation sings hymns of muted
celebration and sips their bottlecaps of blood red wine

THE LEPER WATCHES THE END OF *TWIN PEAKS*

I sit here disappointed by the television
once more   the rods burning out in shapes

I did not want to see   the speakers pumping
sound I did not want to hear   my glass is

a refuge of fermented grapes   a salutation
of tiny bubbles   a certain shade of pale grin

a cool heat   why do I stare at these saturated
pixels again and again   giving myself cataracts

and glaucoma and other forms of eye ulcers
why do I not simply stare into the bottom

of my full glass   let the world be distorted
with myself the director   the glass the

lens so that at least when the time for
disappointment comes   I will be the auteur

THE LEPER RECONSIDERS THE END OF *TWIN PEAKS*

First impressions are difficult to overcome   but not impossible
like infinity from a teapot I have come back around   I too am

trapped in a loop of time   my body deceives me again and again
I fix my heart and sentence my liver to death   I pardon my liver

and my brain cracks open like a trap door   fangs hiding beneath
the fleshy folds   ready to bite through necks   and I long

for the days when there was only a hole in my heart   or a virus
in my blood   I long for coffee and cherry pie   and all the world

offers is a kick in the crotch and a bullet in my foot   I'll always
have my first impression waiting to be dusted off and admired

unchanged   but Now is begging for something new   a second
or third or fourth impression   something like a scream in the night

jarring and eye-opening   something that works no matter the year

SELF-PRESERVATION

I suction the secreted oils from
my skin   devour the thick liquids

of life   pacify my pores so that
they may sing when sweating

I try to live off my own
passions   to speak like

my tongue is on fire
from my own eternal flame.

THE LEPER BURNS HIS MOUTH

The coffee burns my tongue   it blisters my taste buds
all I wanted was to sip and read the news   read about

the orange man and his latest lack of humanity   now
I am injured   now I have yet another thing to worry

about   now the pills will catch on the swollen skin
and be harder to swallow   now I'll choke   what if

there's not enough water   what if the water's twelve
dollars a bottle   what if I'm forced to wash down my

Abilify and blood-pressure meds with motor oil   then
I'll catch fire around the hot television   I'll combust

I'll know what blistering is   but maybe my heart will
run purer   maybe I have a high-octane engine in my

chest and have never really let her rip   maybe I'll burst
through my front door and run circles around all the dirty

white boys on my street   the ones who fly the stars and
bars   the ones who blister at the sound of broken chains

MOWING THE YARD

Dripping with sweat   I push the mower through the tall
wet grass   thinking this would have been easier in a day
or so   after the sun had had its chance to settle its heat

across the cool shadows of the lawn   but this was my
only chance in a week   my sons stand at the front window
learning every way to not mow   to not mangle their future

yards   don't mow in straight rows but around   don't drag
the mower behind you but push it forward   don't rush   let
the experience of mowing move you to breathe the outdoors

let the sparrows feast   young men don't kneel to the whims of
the heat and the weeds   don't do what I do and wallow at nature's
feet   make nature kneel to you   make do with what she gives

THE LEPER DREAMS OF THE OCEAN

I am back on vacation in Myrtle Beach   the dunes
covered in feet and umbrellas   the waves filled with

children and lovers   far out over the water flies a
small plane pulling a banner   *PIRATES*, it says   my

mind plays tricks on me   tells me everyone around me
is plundering my breaths   everyone is looting my

fresh water and nerves   I am panicking like a deck-
hand under siege   I am stealing the light from my

children's eyes   I am marauding over my wife's plans
for fun   I am burning alive beneath the cloudless sky

like the Kraken I flail my limbs around and stomp
across the sand   everyone ducks and sails

away   I sink to the bottom of the ocean
when I awaken   I am covered in salt

THE LEPER CONSIDERS SUNDAY MORNINGS

Here we are looking for gods in the sky   gods in the stars   gods in all
the celestial
bodies   and the gods are busy sipping coffee at the diner   having omelets
with
cheddar and ham   the gods are talking to one another about dropped
handbags

and cracks in sidewalks   about flares and phone calls   about rainfall
records and
regional managers   the gods are wiping their mouths with torn napkins
and putting
too much salt on their food   they're leaving quarters for tips and whispering

to themselves   they're heading out the door and on to the office   muttering
about these desperate windbags   these sacks of bleeding meat   these
sedan
drivers and mud eaters   these fools walking around with their heads
craned up.

THE LEPER CONSIDERS AN ECLIPSE

There is an orange man bending over backwards
to keep a crooked cross flying   there is a car hood

covered in blood   there are statues falling and
folding like wet clay and others standing by

my downtown library   there are white boys in
hipster haircuts carrying backyard bamboo flames

like flag poles   there is a president setting precedent
for a renaissance of hate   beside me on the couch

there is a wife crying   on the floor there are children
roughhousing with the dog   their dark shadows criss-

crossing across the hardwood floor   inside me there is
a certain heat like acid reflux in my bones   out the

front window shadows have fallen all across the street
I'm afraid they'll stay there long after the sun returns.

DRIVING AIMLESSLY

My wife   if you knew how much gas I've burned driving
in circles around New Circle   loops around Richmond
Road   if you knew how many hours I've burned taking

the car around parking lots and gas stations   if you knew
how many times I strapped the toddler into his seat and
drove until he fell asleep just to get a moment's peace

perhaps you would be angry   perhaps you would slap
my face or my bottom   can I tell you how easy it is to
breathe when my foot is pressing down on the pedal

when the city is passing me by   can I tell you how distant
it makes the illnesses feel when I'm hiding in the driver's
seat and counting the miles ticking by on the odometer

can you forgive me the extra expense and wasted
energy   can you understand the weight that drags
behind the bumper instead of resting on my heart?

A LEAF ON THE RIVER

I move off the concrete path   sit on a bench by the river's edge
stretch across the back of the bench   watch the river   a leaf

drifts down the water   does not itself move but is moved
without moving   shifting with the water towards breakers that

will make it move   perhaps violently   perhaps with a finality
that tears it into pieces and scatters it across all directions of

the river so that it can never wholly move again   or perhaps up
and down and then on   maybe side to side and then on like

a brief introduction of movement   maybe with an inversion
or a submersion or merely a half-twist   a slight change of

position before continuing along the river so that old
movements seem like new movements   how it must feel

I think   to move but never choose to move.

THE LEPER HATES

I hate how a nitroglycerin pill feels
beneath my tongue   hate the way my
arm articulates itself with tremulous
tingling   hate how my chest fills with
tension after a heavy meal or when
a stranger says Hello but not when
my blood pressure is in the two-hundreds
hate how doctors shrug in their scrubs
and say *peripheral neuropathy* which
is Latin for *who fucking knows*   hate
checking my pulse every quarter hour
hate popping chalky cylinders twice
a day the blood pill the heartburn pill
the smile pill the don't-be-an-asshole pill
hate the bottles of water   hate the diet after
diet after changing diet   hate the lack
of control   hate feeling like the skin
of a helium balloon stretching more
and more farther and farther tighter
and tighter until I beg for a hemorrhage.

THE LEPER WATCHES *CURIOUS GEORGE*

I watch cartoons with my toddler and ask questions
in my mind   where is this monkey's diaper   does

it shit all over the city/country   and why does no one
beat the hell out of the Man in the Yellow Hat for

letting his wild animal fuck up their days   I intend to
ask the baby this   he sits enamored   no more aware

that monkeys cannot float on kites than I am aware
that space is more than a four-dimensional construct

there are many worlds with many monkeys   there are
many universes with many banana-loving men   there

are worlds where I can breathe without my heart skipping
there are galaxies where my insanity is really sanity

squared   there are Earths where my son knows the
patience of animated farmers instead of aggravated daddies

there is a world where he is free and I am free
and we are free together to climb asteroids and explore

the cosmos and speak without collapsing like stars

WASHING THE DOG

Her urine flows hot from the bottom of her to the bottom of me
my toes soaked and sticky and smelling like rotted fruit   this is
a struggle   a fight   a battle   a war for a house free of parasites

my wife found a flea on my toddler's head and that was it
for smelling like wet dead wood   on my to-do list *wash the dog*
beside *take my books back to the library* and *fold the cutlery*

and *bite yourself*   I throw the dog into the tub and turn on the
shower head and spray her top to bottom   my foot cools and
smells of defense mechanisms   I nearly drown her in hot water

and soap   the fleas flow into the drain   the dog moans and shakes
herself free of water   her only pleasure the drenched t-shirt
on my chest   mine the dank smell of a scratched-out phrase

I heave while bending over the tub   I feel my stomach turn at
the stench of her piss   I feel my heart try to jump out of my chest
I am not made for this   I am not designed to hold down this

pitiful bitch and scrub the bugs from her skin   my heart is too full
of blood and plaque   my face is too strained   my arteries stretched
too tight   I may die here in the bathroom   I may lose my life

and then it's over and she's sprinting in circles around
the house while I clutch my sternum and curse loudly
with flowers blooming in my eyes   neon breathless flowers

Sean L **Corbin** holds an MFA in Creative Writing from the University of Kentucky, as well as degrees in English and Creative Writing from Morehead State University. His poems, prose, and literary reviews have appeared in *Still: The Journal, Crow Hollow, Poetry Fix, CircleShow, Door is a Jar, Solidago, little leo, Vine Leaves, Vinyl Poetry, Inscape,* and *JMWW*. Sean currently lives in Lexington, Kentucky, with his wife, the writer Amanda Kelley Corbin, and their two sons. He currently works as a freelance writer, teacher, and visual artist. His work and musings can be found at seanlcorbin.wordpress.com.

www.ingramcontent.com/pod-product-compliance
Lightning Source LLC
LaVergne TN
LVHW021123080426
835510LV00021B/3294

* 9 7 8 1 6 3 5 3 4 6 5 0 3 *